P9-DEV-443

3/04

The Library of the Middle Ages™

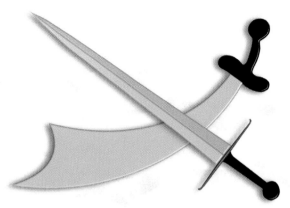

The First Crusade

The Capture of Jerusalem in AD 1099

Susan B. Edgington

Published in 2004 by The Rosen Publishing Group, Inc.
29 East 21st Street, New York, NY 10010

Copyright © 2004 by The Rosen Publishing Group, Inc.

First Edition

Library of Congress Cataloging-in-Publication Data

Edgington, Susan.
The first crusade: the capture of Jerusalem in AD 1099/Susan B. Edgington.—1st ed.
    v. cm.—(The library of the Middle Ages)
Includes bibliographical references and index.
Contents: Pope Urban's speech—The first departures—The official armies—Asia Minor—Antioch.
ISBN 0-8239-4214-7 (library binding)
1. Crusades—First, 1096–1099—Juvenile literature.
2. Church history—Middle Ages, 600–1500—Juvenile literature.
3. Jerusalem—History—Latin Kingdom, 1099–1244—Juvenile literature. [1. Crusades—First, 1096–1099. 2. Jerusalem—History.]
I. Title. II. Series.
D161.2.E34 2003
956'.014—dc21

2002155345

Manufactured in the United States of America

Table of Contents

Pope Urban II addresses the faithful at the Council of Clermont in AD 1095, from a fifteenth-century illuminated manuscript. The pope called upon the princes of Europe to defend the Byzantine Empire and rescue the Holy Land from the Turks.

Pope Urban's Speech

At the end of November in AD 1095, Pope Urban II delivered a carefully prepared speech to a large audience in the city of Clermont in southern France. In fact, so many people had gathered to hear him that he had to hold the meeting out in the open air. We do not know precisely what he said, but the response was extraordinary and the consequences far-reaching. This speech can be called the beginning of the crusading movement.

Earlier in the same year, the pope had received a letter from the Byzantine emperor, Alexius Comnenus, in Constantinople. The letter asked Pope Urban and the leaders of western Europe to send troops to help the emperor to defend his lands against the Seljuk Turks. The Turks had conquered most of Asia Minor, and the emperor was afraid that they would attack Constantinople itself. With the aid of western knights, he hoped to drive them back and to recapture some of the towns and lands that had been lost.

The pope had his own reasons for supporting the emperor's request. It would be a friendly gesture that might help to mend relations between the eastern and western parts of the Christian church, which had been strained since a dispute in 1054. Urban also wanted to impose his authority over the lords of western Europe, who had challenged the pope's right to have a say in the appointment of bishops and other matters. This was also an opportunity to do something about the constant warfare between the knights who were the sons of those same lords. If these younger men could be persuaded to join up for an expedition to the East, then some sort of peace could be imposed on their lands at home.

Liberate Jerusalem!

Pope Urban could not explain these deeper political motives to his audience. He needed to find another way to make the expedition attractive to the knights and their followers. According to a cleric named Robert the Monk who heard his speech, the pope did not concentrate on the prospect of fighting for the Byzantine emperor. Instead, he spoke movingly about Jerusalem, calling it "the navel of the world," that is, the world's very center. He described how this holy city, where Jesus had lived and died, was in the hands of the enemy Turks, and how Christians were being persecuted and prevented from worshiping there. He called on his listeners to liberate Jerusalem, and he flattered them by telling them that they, the Franks, were the bravest knights in the world. He also promised them that the journey would be a penance and would bring them remission—that is, forgiveness—of their sins. Many who heard him must have been attracted by the idea of fighting (which was all a knight was really trained for) and, instead of earning the disapproval of the Church, gaining a place in heaven.

The pope inspired the knights by focusing on Jerusalem. Many people at the time honored Jesus and the saints by seeking out their shrines. They hoped, most of all, to go on one of the great pilgrimages, especially a journey to Jerusalem. An expedition to rescue the so-called holy places of Jerusalem would be the most glorious pilgrimage of all. People were also aware that, as it said in the Bible, Jesus would reappear in glory after a thousand years. How could this happen if the holy city were in the hands of unbelievers? The ideas of penance and pilgrimage were reinforced by another ritual. Knights were invited to literally "take the cross" and to pin onto their shoulders strips of cloth in the shape of a cross, which they would wear until the end of the expedition.

Pope Urban had managed the meeting in another way. He had primed a great lord, Raymond of Toulouse, to be among the first to take the cross. Raymond was an elderly man with grown-up children whom he could leave in charge of his lands in southern France. He also had a history of fighting the Muslims, not in the East but in Spain. Many of Raymond's vassals, or tenants, followed his lead and enlisted for the expedition. The pope's official representative, Bishop Adhemar of Le Puy, was to travel with Raymond when they left for the East. Another group who volunteered for the expedition came from the northern French lands. Among their leaders were Robert Curthose, the son of William the Conqueror who had become king of England in 1066; Stephen of Blois, who was married to William the Conqueror's daughter; Hugh, the brother of the king of France; and Robert of Flanders. To allow others the

Knights in combat, from a twelfth-century German book illustration. Training for war was the principal occupation of noblemen who ruled Europe as a military caste.

opportunity to join the campaign, Pope Urban sent preachers out to publicize it.

Thus far, the pope was in charge of the expedition. He further took care to set the date for departure on the Feast of the Assumption, August 15, 1096. A date of almost nine months away was chosen to allow his knightly recruits to return home and make proper preparations. The knights needed to equip themselves for the long journey, taking horses, mules, or donkeys as pack animals. They needed clothing and body armor. The armor they needed included chain mail, composed of tiny rings of metal riveted together, or padded leather. They would also need metal helmets. They would need to obtain weapons, including lances for riding down the enemy when on horseback and swords for fighting once dismounted. They would need portable wealth, like coins or jewels, to be able to replace equipment that was lost or destroyed. And they would need as much food as they could carry. In addition, most knights would be supported by a squire, and they might also take servants to look after them and their horses. Some were accompanied by their wives or other kinswomen, who would in turn need to take maidservants. Every contingent needed to have cooks, washerwomen, blacksmiths, carpenters, armorers, and various other skilled craftsmen.

As well as making preparations for the journey, the lords needed to ensure that their lands and families would be safe while they were away. Some, like Raymond, were able to leave them in the hands of a grown son. Others made a deal with the local monastery or abbey for the monks to protect their estates while they were away. The monks ensured that the estates were not attacked by neighboring lords and that they continued to be farmed productively. These agreements were sometimes written down, and they tell us a little about the knights' expectations. For example, the charter might note that the knight expected to be away for no more than two years on the journey to Jerusalem.

The date the pope set for departure in mid-August was carefully chosen. The armies would set off after the harvest was in, taking enough food supplies to see them well on their way, while the lands they were passing through would also have plentiful provisions for them to buy. The armies would take different routes, which meant that

Peter the Hermit leads his followers to the Holy Land, from a fourteenth-century manuscript illumination. The illustration shows that women as well as soldiers accompanied him. Most came to a terrible end.

the burden of provisioning them was borne by different peoples in different areas. They would rendezvous in Constantinople in the late fall to spend the winter as the eastern emperor's guests, before setting out to fight for him when the campaigning

The Middle East was a holy place for worshippers of Islam as well as Christians. Here, from a thirteenth-century Arab manuscript, Muslims make a pilgrimage to Mecca to receive religious instruction.

season began the following spring.

The First Departures

The pope's plan was to enlist an army of trained and well-equipped knights to travel to Constantinople and take their orders from the emperor there. However, he completely underestimated the impact of putting Jerusalem at the heart of his speech. He fired the enthusiasm of many more people than his intended audience. All over western Europe, ordinary people as well as trained knights were eager to undertake a great pilgrimage and to liberate Jerusalem.

Old and young, men and women, laypeople and clerics, rich and poor—all sorts of people responded as clerics spread the message across western Europe. The most famous of these preachers was Peter the Hermit. People from towns and villages in northern France flocked to hear Peter tell how he had gone on the pilgrimage to Jerusalem and how, when he arrived in the city, he was beaten up and prevented from praying in the Church of the Holy Sepulchre. Peter told them that he had sought out the patriarch, or head of the church, of Jerusalem, who had said how difficult it was becoming for pilgrims now that the Turks governed Jerusalem. The patriarch gave Peter a letter for the pope, asking for help to make the holy places in Jerusalem safe for western visitors. So according to Peter's story, it was he who had put the idea of liberating Jerusalem into Pope Urban's mind.

Peter must have been a charismatic preacher, for in spite of his appearance (one of his critics said he resembled his own mule), he soon gathered an army of supporters who wanted to follow him to Jerusalem. There were a few knights among them, but most were from ordinary families: peasants and tradespeople who believed that they were doing God's work and that they did not need weapons because God would protect them. Nor did they need to worry about supplies, because God would provide for them. There were probably less pious people, too, who were looking for adventure, wanted to escape the daily grind of a peasant's work, or were on the run from the law or from people they owed money to. But they were all Christian believers who undertook the journey as a pilgrimage to receive forgiveness for their sins.

Because they believed that God would look after them, they could not be persuaded to wait for the official departure date in August. They wanted to start their journey as soon as the weather improved and the routes became passable in the

King Solomon reads the Torah, from a thirteenth-century Hebrew Bible. Jewish communities throughout Europe were persecuted during the Crusades.

spring of 1096. We do not know how many there were in this unusual army. Certainly thousands set off from northern France and the Low Countries, the region around modern-day Belgium, Luxembourg, and Holland. Some of them dropped out when they realized how difficult the journey would be. Probably many of them, and not only the children, had no idea of the vast distances involved. The chronicler Guibert of Nogent reports that as any city or castle appeared on the horizon the cry went up, "Is that Jerusalem? Are we nearly there?" They found it difficult to obtain supplies, for they were dependent on the generosity of peasants like themselves, who had very little at this time of the year. Sometimes they got into fights in the market towns because they helped themselves to the food they needed, and some pilgrims, as well as the people they attacked, were killed and injured.

Nevertheless, it was still a large if ragged army that entered the territory of the Byzantine Empire in the summer of 1096. The emperor had been expecting an army of rein- forcements that was made up of professional soldiers. The astonishment of the Byzantines at the approach of Peter the Hermit's followers still echoes in the words the emperor's daughter Anna later wrote in her biography. Anna described these crusaders as "an unarmed crowd, including even women and children and outnumbering the sand or the stars." This rabble was of little use to the emperor. He was concerned about keeping them out of his great capital city of Constantinople, because he knew that they had caused trouble in more distant parts of his lands. He decided to ferry them across the straits that divided the city, which was on the European shore, from Asia Minor. He told them to make a camp there and to wait for the official army of sol- diers that he knew by now was on its way. He would supply them in the meantime.

Although there had been some unruly behavior on the journey, Peter had done well up to this point in keeping his rabble together and preventing them from getting into worse trouble. However, while he was absent from the camp negoti- ating with the emperor in Constantinople for the supplies they needed, his followers started to fight among themselves. The rivalry between gangs of young men, Franks and Germans, led them to provoke the Turks, who descended on the camp and destroyed it. They killed the men of fighting

This twelfth-century church is in Trier, Germany, one of the cities where mobs of crusaders attacked the Jewish community. Local bishops tried to protect the Jewish people, but they were not successful.

age and anyone too old or young to be of value to them, and took the rest captive. Peter's pilgrimage, which had started with an upsurge of faith, ended in disaster.

Attacks on the Jews

While Peter's followers at least managed to reach Constantinople, other groups failed to get even that far. Some of them, including a gang led by Count Emich, turned on the Jews in the cities of the Rhineland in what is now modern Germany. Their excuse for this was that the Jews were the enemy of Christ. They did not see why they needed to go all the way to Jerusalem to kill Christ's enemies when these Jews were living among them. But the leaders were almost certainly motivated by greed as well. Jews had been living in the towns of western Europe for centuries. According to the requirements of their religion, ten adult men were needed to sustain a synagogue. They also had to live within walking distance of it. This meant that the Jews in any city would inhabit their own district, within which they kept to their own customs, including their distinctive ways of dressing and speaking. Through hard work and by supporting one another within their communities, many had become wealthy, and, unlike Christians, were not barred by their religious beliefs from lending money in return for interest. They had accumulated wealth in gold and coinage that the would-be pilgrims coveted for financing their journey. The Jews were not protected by their local Christian neighbors, many of whom probably owed them money and hoped to see their debts disappear. In some places, the townspeople joined the bands of thugs who were attacking the Jews.

The Jews were attacked in the German cities of Speyer, Worms, Mainz, Cologne, and Trier. Their first response was usually to seek refuge with the local bishop because the attacks were not the official policy of the Catholic Church. In Speyer the bishop succeeded in protecting them, but elsewhere there were horrible scenes of forced conversion and murder. Count Emich's men broke into the bishop's palace in Mainz to find that Jewish men, women, and children had killed themselves rather than surrender. Although the authorities condemned the attacks, they were unable to prevent them. Most disturbing of all was that the violence against the Jews in 1096 was only the beginning. Crusaders turned on the Jews fifty years later during the Second Crusade and in future crusades after that.

Beside the sinister gangs who attacked the Jews, other groups seem merely foolish. One little band followed a goose, convinced that it was inspired by the Holy Spirit. Another group was led by a goat. They stood no chance of reaching Constantinople, let alone completing their pilgrimage to Jerusalem.

Knights setting out on a crusade, from a twelfth-century French painting. They are wearing crosses on their tunics.

The Armies March

ount Raymond had spent the winter putting his affairs in order so that he could set out in August. He probably did not expect to return to his lands, anticipating establishing a new realm for himself in the Holy Land. He took with him his second wife, as well as a great number of knights, along with squires and servants. This army from southern France was the biggest one, and Raymond probably thought of himself as the overall leader of the combined expedition, especially since the pope's legate, or representative, Bishop Adhemar, traveled with him. They marched from southern France down through Italy and boarded ships from Bari to cross the Adriatic Sea to Durazzo, part of the Byzantine Empire.

There they joined forces with the second major contingent, which included the soldiers of the northern French nobles Robert of Flanders, Robert of Normandy, Stephen of Blois, and Hugh of France. The northern nobles had taken a different route along the Adriatic coast. Their army was also accompanied by many noncombatants. We know from a few surviving letters that Pope Urban was worried that his recruitment had been overly successful. He tried to stop monks and priests from going without the permission of their abbots and bishops. News of the problems of the "unofficial" armies of Peter the Hermit and others had probably reached him.

It was not only noncombatants that the pope had to worry about. Two members of the nobility responded to his appeal without invitation, and the pope was probably not pleased. The first was Duke Godfrey of Bouillon (in present-day Belgium). Godfrey was a loyal supporter of the German king, who was no friend of the pope. In fact, Godfrey had been with the German king when he besieged the pope in Rome only a few years earlier. Nevertheless, Godfrey seems to have been a pious man. He traveled with his elder brother, Eustace, who was a less impressive character, his brother Baldwin, and many of their vassals. Godfrey followed the same route as Peter the Hermit, using the old Roman roads and following first the Rhine and then the Danube River valley. He found that his journey was made more difficult because of the trouble caused by the unofficial armies, especially in Hungary. Emich's followers had been wiped out there, and the local king was understandably reluctant to allow Godfrey and his army to pass through until he was granted hostages to ensure their good behavior. So Godfrey handed over his brother Baldwin and Baldwin's wife.

The fourth major contingent was led by Bohemond, the most flamboyant character of all. If we are to believe his chronicler, the anonymous author of *The Deeds of the Franks*, Bohemond did not receive an invitation to join. He had heard about the great expedition while he was engaged in besieging Amalfi in southern Italy. When he found out about the campaign, he vowed to go. Bohemond's history and his later actions suggest that he may have had reasons other than religious fervor for traveling to Constantinople. Bohemond's ancestors were Norman adventurers who had conquered southern Italy. As one of several younger sons who would not inherit his family's estates, he was ambitious to carve out his own territory, either in Italy or farther afield. His decision to take an army to the East was ominous for the expedition, because he and his father had already waged war on the Byzantine emperor during the 1080s. Now the Eastern emperor was expected to believe that Bohemond would be content to serve under his leadership in a fight to defend the empire against the Turks.

At Constantinople

Put on his guard by his experience with the followers of Peter the Hermit, the Byzantine emperor prepared a plan for dealing with the approaching armies. They were expecting to spend the winter in Constantinople before advancing against the Turks and making the journey to Jerusalem in the spring of 1097. The emperor wanted to prevent the different contingents from joining together and possibly conspiring against him, so he dealt with each of them separately. He was careful to keep the armies outside the city walls, admitting only their leaders to his palace. There he put on a splendid show of wealth and power to impress them, and he gave them generous gifts of gold, silver, and precious silk. Having softened them up, he then asked them to swear an oath to him. He wanted them to promise that they would serve under his

Emperor Alexius Comnenus, leader of the Byzantine Empire at the time of the First Crusade. Done in the Eastern style, this work is a mosaic made of inlaid colored stones, rather than a painting or fresco typical of Western artists.

command and restore to him any lands and castles they captured that had previously belonged to the Byzantine Empire. An oath at that time was as good as a legal contract is today. For his part, the emperor promised to send an army to fight alongside the westerners and also to supply them with food and equipment.

The wary Byzantine emperor did not have it all his own way. In fact, there was trouble even before the majority of the crusaders arrived in Constantinople, because a rumor spread that Hugh of France had been taken prisoner by the emperor. Later on, Godfrey's soldiers caused trouble in their camp outside the walls. And although most of the leaders took the oath without any protest, Raymond insisted on a modified version, while Bohemond's nephew, Tancred, managed to evade taking it at all. Bohemond himself took the oath without having any reservations, but he may already have been plotting how to avoid keeping it. This is what Anna, the Byzantine emperor's daughter, believed. Bohemond made a strong impression on her, although she was only fourteen years old at the time and did not write about the meeting until forty years later. She described him as a giant among men, blond and barbaric.

This is a mid-sixteenth-century map of the great city of Constantinople (now Istanbul), capital of the Eastern Roman Empire.

Whatever his reservations about these strange allies, the emperor had to work with them. No doubt it seemed a long winter, with the constant anxiety of keeping the peace in the crusaders' camps and supplying adequate provisions for so many people. In the spring of 1097, the campaigning season began. The emperor sent the crusaders across the straits to besiege

The conquest of Nicaea on June 20, 1097, from a fourteenth-century Venetian manuscript. Nicaea was the first city in Asia Minor captured from the Turks by the crusaders.

Nicaea, which was his first strategic objective. The city of Nicaea was in Asia Minor but only a short distance from Constantinople. It had been in the hands of the Seljuk Turks since 1086. The Seljuks had a warlike history and held three great cities that were important in Christian history: Nicaea, Antioch, and Jerusalem. The emperor, however, was more concerned about Nicaea because the city was so close to his capital.

The Siege of Nicaea

When the Byzantine emperor dispatched the crusading armies across the straits to besiege Nicaea, they were accompanied by his general, Taticius. At the same time, another one of his generals, Boutoumites, opened negotiations with the Turks who commanded the city. This twofold approach was standard practice in siege warfare. The threat of military force was used in combination with inducements to surrender.

The crusaders knew about sieges from their experiences in western Europe. In fact, although we may think of medieval wars as consisting of knights charging into battle on horseback, most of their campaigning involved sieges. This is when the beseiged took refuge inside a fortress—it could be a castle or a walled town—that the attackers wanted to seize from them. There were one or two complications. The attackers would not want to spend too long a time encamped around the fortress, because they were in enemy territory and would find it difficult to get supplies. They also wanted to capture the fortress without damaging it too much, because it was very likely that they would need to take refuge inside it themselves. Nevertheless, the classic way to begin a siege was to blockade the town. This meant surrounding it and attempting to prevent people from getting out and supplies from getting in. Although a long siege was risky, attackers had to make a show of settling in for as long as it might take to starve the enemy out.

The attackers would build siege engines to look as menacing as possible and to try to persuade the enemy that they might as well give up. These siege engines were of three main types. There were throwing machines and catapults, called mangonels or trebuchets, which hurled rocks and other unpleasant things, like dead animals or human heads, over the walls to intimidate the defenders. There were battering rams for breaking down the gates of the fortress, and there were siege towers, which contained ladders protected from arrows that could be brought up to the

Delacite denique fachiez que le fu
coniz leneschie deni comede Afef lem
pereref coftantine la fuft ofter delpooir Acel

The siege of Nicaea, from a twelfth-century French manuscript. The crusaders used their catapults to lob the heads of dead Turks over the city's walls to demoralize their enemies.

walls to enable the attackers to climb onto the tops of them. The crusaders used all of these different engines during their campaign, and sometimes they also dug mines beneath the enemy walls. These were not tunnels to get them inside the city, but a way of bringing a section of the wall down. Once the miners had dug underneath the foundations of the wall, they would shore up their mine with timbers and then retreat before they set fire to the timbers. The pit props would burn and collapse, bringing down the wall with them.

Although the blockaders would make a great show of being prepared to use all these methods of attack, the real point was to convince the defenders of the fortress that they could not win and to induce them to surrender. Then the attackers would gain the fortress more or less intact and without too much loss of life or discomfort. The earlier the defenders surrendered, the better the terms they could get, so that their lives and property might be protected, while they knew that if the fortress was taken by assault there would be no mercy shown to them. So there were always elements of bluff and calculation involved in a siege.

Nicaea was a strongly walled city with a large lake on the western side. This prevented the crusaders from closing the blockade, and it allowed the defenders to come and go as they pleased. They brought in supplies under the crusaders' noses, and the governor's family was shipped to safety without the crusaders being able to do anything about it. This standoff was broken only when the emperor had ships brought overland—the Franks pulled them from the sea on rollers—and floated them on the lake. When the Turks woke up and saw them one morning, they thought at first that supply ships had arrived, but they soon realized that the crusaders had succeeded in closing the blockade. This persuaded them to surrender. However, they yielded to the Byzantine emperor, not to the crusaders, and the Frankish soldiers were disappointed because they were not allowed to loot the town. This event can be seen as the beginning of their disillusionment with the Byzantine Empire, which later turned into outright hostility.

Marching Through Asia Minor

Once the Byzantine emperor had possession of Nicaea, he was anxious for the crusaders to move off. He did not want them to cause trouble within the captured city. So they set off in the middle of summer in 1097, on their way through the mountains of Asia Minor in the direction of Antioch. Because of their great numbers—it has been estimated that there were more than fifty thousand people on the expedition at this stage—and the narrowness of the roads through the valleys and passes, their lines became very stretched out, which made them vulnerable to ambushes by the Turks.

The most serious attack occurred in a city called Dorylaeum. Initially, the crusaders were astonished by the Turkish tactics. In their own lands, pitched battles were fought according to certain conventions. The opposing ranks of knights rode at one another, and each knight attempted to unhorse an opponent by striking him with a lance. The defeated knight might not be killed but taken prisoner and held for ransom. The Turks fought in a vastly different way. They used mounted archers who rode down the mountain slopes, releasing arrow after arrow as they rode past the more static crusaders, so that arrows rained down on them. The Turks also made a great din with bugles and drums and war cries.

Frightened though they were by these tactics, the crusaders stood firm at Dorylaeum and fought back until reinforcements arrived and the Turks retreated. It seemed to the crusaders a splendid victory, and they were in good spirits. They had captured a great city and won their first real battle against the Turks. It seemed to them that it would only be a matter of a few weeks before they reached Jerusalem.

Two Islamic warriors jousting, from a twelfth-century Egyptian manuscript. The style of combat was similar to that of western Europe, but these men did not wear armor or carry shields.

But by now it was July. The sun was scorching down. After the ambush at Dorylaeum, the leaders were anxious to prevent their lines from becoming too long again. This meant moving at the speed of the slowest contingents, and soon their water supplies ran low. People started to die of thirst, and so did their animals. The knights had horses and pack animals, and some of them had taken dogs and hawks with them, not as pets but to hunt for food for their masters. All of them were affected by the heat and thirst. At one point, the crusaders found a polluted river and some of the people could not be held back from drinking the water, and they, too, died. Later on, as they came nearer to Antioch, some of the knights threw away their armor and tried to sell their weapons to make the journey easier, now that they did not have pack animals to carry the heavy baggage.

Baldwin's Armenian Adventure

Northeast of the crusaders' route through Asia Minor was the land of Armenia, with its capital city at Edessa. The inhabitants of Armenia were Christians, although they had their own customs and did not accept the pope as their leader. The Seljuk Turks had captured Edessa from the Byzantines. So when the inhabitants heard of the approach of a great Christian army from western Europe, they saw an opportunity to ask for help to overthrow their Turkish rulers, without having to submit to Byzantine rule again. They may have thought that a western prince could be easily manipulated. So the people of Edessa sent scouts and envoys to the crusaders to ask them for help against the Turks.

Two of the younger nobles, who were probably feeling frustrated by the slow progress of the expedition toward Antioch, saw the opportunity for a fast-moving thrust north. They were Baldwin, Duke Godfrey's younger brother, and Tancred, the nephew of Bohemond. They may have been encouraged by their older relatives, who could see the advantages of establishing an ally and possibly a supply base not far from Antioch. However, the young men were rivals rather than companions, and it was Baldwin who had the greater success. He was invited by the elders of Edessa to come to the city, and there he was made coruler with the prince, Thoros. Not long afterward, the elders of the city were plotting again, this time to depose Thoros and make Baldwin sole ruler. We do not know how far Baldwin himself was implicated in the conspiracy. When Thoros took refuge in a tower, Baldwin allowed him to escape through the second-floor window, and Thoros was shot through with arrows before he reached the ground.

Baldwin stayed in Edessa with a few of his followers while the rest of the army marched on to Antioch. His first wife had died during the hard march through Asia Minor, so he married the daughter of one of the Armenian elders. During the rest of the campaign, Edessa was a source of support to the main crusading army. Baldwin sent horses and other equipment to his brother Godfrey during the siege of Antioch, and when there was an outbreak of disease in the camp, Godfrey took refuge in the healthier air of Armenia. The crusader-ruled city of Edessa was not offered to the Byzantine emperor, but it became the first crusader kingdom in Asia Minor.

The attack on Antioch in 1098, from a thirteenth-century history by William of Tyre

Antioch

he recapture of Antioch may have been the Byzantine emperor's main objective from the beginning. An ancient and cosmopolitan city, it had been a center of learning and trade in the great days of the Roman Empire. Later, it was captured by the Persians and then by the Arabs, who returned it to the Byzantines in AD 969. But it was lost to the Turks in 1085. In spite of the city's contested history and many massive earthquakes, it remained strongly fortified. For the crusaders, it was the gateway to Jerusalem, controlling the route between the mountains and the sea. So when they arrived at the city in October 1097, they settled down to besiege it.

It was immediately obvious that this siege was going to take much longer than the one at Nicaea. Antioch was a much larger city, and approximately seven miles of wall needed to be blockaded. Even if the crusaders had had the numbers to do this, they would have had trouble assaulting the steep slopes. The eastern part of the walls ran along the top of a mountain ridge, with the citadel on the top of Mount Silpius overlooking the town and the mountain paths leading into the interior of Syria. The rough mountain slopes meant that sheep and goats could be grazed within the city walls, and there were small farms and orchards within the walls, too, as well as springs and wells to provide water. So Antioch was in a position to withstand a long siege.

The crusaders encamped on the more level ground north and west of the city, where the Orontes River skirted the city walls. It was the onset of winter, and they were unprepared for the cold and rain that rotted their tents and loosened their bowstrings. Supplies had to be brought from the nearby port of St. Symeon along roads that were exposed to the ambushes of the Turks, and hunger was constant. Also, because of the conditions in the camps, there were outbreaks of disease. Meanwhile, the Turkish defenders had sufficient food and drink and taunted the crusaders with sorties and raids. They were also able to summon assistance from Turkish allies, who attacked the crusaders and had to be fought off. Some of the crusaders decided the situation was hopeless and they deserted, even though their chances of reaching home were not good.

The Capture of Antioch

By spring it was clear that the city was not going to be forced to surrender, either by a show of force or by starvation. Moreover, Turkish allies were preparing to bring up an enormous army to relieve the city. The leaders who made up the war council were themselves becoming desperate. The

The siege of Antioch, from a fifteenth-century French illuminated manuscript. The crusaders breached the outer walls and captured the city on June 3, 1098, but it was two more weeks before they drove off a supporting Turkish army and captured the central citadel.

Come antioche fut prinse des crines et puis
asseutee des turce   iiij xx

Ledseigneur ost vint a grant force
ou val dantioche qui est la mai
stre cite de syrie tout sermie En
ceste cite est laquarte plus noble de toutes
Cest apres rome constantinoble et alixadrie
Et la est ung fleune qui radis estoit dit orons

A herd of camels, from a thirteenth-century Arab manuscript

Byzantine emperor's representative, Taticius, had withdrawn with his troops, giving Bohemond his opportunity. Bohemond told the other leaders that the emperor had now broken his side of the bargain, and so they were no longer under any obligation to hand over Antioch to him if it could be taken. Some of the leaders disagreed with him, including Godfrey and Raymond. Nevertheless, the prospect of capturing the city must have seemed remote, so they told Bohemond that if he could enable them to capture Antioch, he could keep it.

In fact, Bohemond already had a plan for capturing the city. He had contacted one of its citizens, who commanded three towers in the city walls, and persuaded him to betray Antioch. How he managed this is not entirely clear, but according to one account, Bohemond held the commander's son as hostage. According to another account, the commander was converted to Christianity. And according to yet another account, he was bribed. In any event, he agreed to let down a ladder from the walls during the night so that the crusaders could climb into the city. So by means of treachery and cunning, Antioch was captured on June 3, 1098.

It was not a moment too soon. The crusaders scarcely had time to occupy the city before the combined Turkish army, led by General Kerbogha, arrived. The Franks now found that they were the ones under siege. Worse still, they had failed to capture the citadel, which commanded the walls of the city in such a way that the Turkish garrison inside could easily communicate with the Turkish army outside. And worst of all, their hopes of a Byzantine army arriving in time to save them were dashed when Stephen of Blois, who had deserted them on the eve of the capture of the city, met the emperor and persuaded him that the situation was hopeless and that he should turn back. The crusaders' numbers, already reduced by battle casualties and desertion, were being worn down daily by famine and disease.

The only thing that could save them was a miracle, and that is exactly what happened—or was arranged to happen. A peasant soldier dreamt that the very lance that had pierced Christ's side when he was on the cross was buried in one of the churches in Antioch. When he dug, he found a lance. Many people said that the whole episode was a fraud, but the leaders recognized that such a holy relic was exactly what they needed to boost the army's morale and convince them that God was fighting for them.

The Turks attack the army of Bohemond as it crosses the Wardar River, from a fifteenth-century French illuminated manuscript. The defeat of this Turkish army secured Antioch for the crusaders.

Two weeks later, the tattered remnants of the crusader army followed the Holy Lance into battle. They were weakened by famine and disease. So many of their horses had died that some knights were mounted on donkeys or mules, and others were fighting on foot. According to one account, women, old men, and priests formed battalions to fight alongside the knights. As they lined up for battle, they were under observation from the citadel. The Turkish garrison signalled the coming Christian attack to General Kerbogha. And yet, against all odds, this ragtag army succeeded in defeating the massed forces of the Turks. The crusaders themselves recognized their victory as a miracle, and stories circulated afterward that saints had appeared and fought on the side of the Christians. Sheer desperation was probably the real cause of victory, because the crusaders charged the center of the Turkish lines and could not be turned aside. Bohemond credited his leadership for the victory, and after the battle was won and the citadel finally captured, he claimed the right to become Antioch's commander. Thus, Antioch became the second crusader kingdom.

The crusaders were unfit to set out for Jerusalem immediately. It was now the middle of summer, and they were still weak and afflicted by disease. On August 1, 1098, they suffered a great loss when Bishop Adhemar died. Although he was a churchman, he was also a good leader and one of the few people who might have been able to keep the army's leaders from quarreling among themselves. After he died the rivalry between Bohemond and Raymond became more open, and this was one reason Raymond was reluctant to move on. He busied himself in the country around Antioch, occupying small towns and fortresses.

One of the nearby towns, called Ma'arrat, was the scene of an infamous incident that was reported in all the chronicles. The crusaders became cannibals. The men responsible were a gang of renegade ruffians who called themselves Tafurs. These men were hungry, of course, but they also seem to have been practicing a cruel kind of psychological warfare, since they carried out the crime in full view of the garrison.

The ordinary soldiers became weary of the time wasted at Antioch and demanded that the leaders carry on to Jerusalem. The leaders agreed they would start in November, when the weather was cooler and healthier. However, it was not until the following spring of 1099 that the army continued on its way.

The taking of Jerusalem in 1099, from a fourteenth-century French manuscript. The crusaders use ladders to assault the higher levels of the fortress, where the Saracens hold Christian martyrs as hostages.

The Capture of Jerusalem

The crusaders had to choose whether to march south along the coast, a route that occasionally became very narrow and difficult, or to risk marching along the inland route, where the danger was from the Turks. They chose the coastal route. They then had to decide whether to attack the towns that stood in their way. This could prove costly in both time and manpower, as they found out when Raymond besieged the town of Arqa without success. After that they realized that it was more sensible to make truce agreements with the emirs, or chieftains, of each city. The crusaders would bypass the towns and in return receive money and provisions to speed them on their way. The exception was Jaffa, the nearest port to Jerusalem, which they found abandoned by the enemy and were able to garrison. Further inland, Tancred and a few companions arrived in Bethlehem, where they were welcomed by its Christian inhabitants.

The crusaders had taken so long to march this far that the political situation in Asia Minor had changed. During the previous summer of 1098, while the crusaders

Pages of the Koran from a thirteenth-century Seljuk Turk manuscript

were still held up at Antioch, Saracens from Egypt had succeeded in capturing Jerusalem from the Turks. Although the Saracens were also Muslim, they were not at this time enemies of the Byzantines, as the Turks were. In fact, they had sent ambassadors to the crusaders proposing a peace that would allow the Christians access to Jerusalem. The crusaders were not prepared to listen, maybe because they were suspicious of the Saracens' alliance with the Byzantines or maybe because they could not entertain the idea of coming so far and suffering so much and not capturing Jerusalem. So the Saracen commander in Jerusalem prepared for their

Crusader knights battle the Moors, from a fourteenth-century French manuscript illustration

arrival by expelling the Christians, blocking or poisoning wells and other sources of water around the city, and barring the gates in preparation for a siege.

On June 7, 1099, the crusader army saw Jerusalem for the first time. They wept, prayed, and gave thanks. Then they set about establishing a siege. The city was well fortified, and the crusader numbers were too few to surround it completely. So they concentrated on the southwest side of the city, where Raymond encamped, and the northern wall, where Godfrey prepared for an assault. Within a week they had attempted an attack, but it failed because they did not

The Dome of the Rock, in the al-Aqsa Mosque, in Jerusalem. Built in AD 687 to commemorate the journey to heaven made by the prophet Muhammad from this spot, it was one of the prizes captured by the crusaders.

have wood to build siege towers. Just then, by good fortune, Genoese ships sailed into the newly garrisoned harbor at Jaffa. The captains agreed to sacrifice the ships to the Christian war effort. However, it took time to build siege engines and scaling ladders, and the heat and lack of water were beginning to sap the crusaders' strength. They knew that an army was on its way from Egypt to assist the defenders of Jerusalem, and they worried they might fail when the great prize was almost within their grasp. As usual in times of crisis, they turned to prayer, and a three-day fast was declared, with a penitential procession around the walls. This renewed their faith and their fighting spirit, and a week later they launched an assault on the city.

It was Godfrey's men who were first in, going over the wall by means of a siege tower. They opened the gates to their comrades, and the crusaders rushed into Jerusalem, killing the inhabitants, regardless of religion, age, or sex, with terrible bloodshed. Only the city's commander and his immediate followers escaped, by handing over the citadel to Raymond. Godfrey is said to have held back from the slaughter and to have completed his pilgrimage by praying in the Church of the Holy Sepulchre. Thus, when the killing ceased, these two leaders—Raymond and Godfrey— each had a claim to become ruler of the city. It was urgent that the matter of its future government be settled because the Egyptian army was by now encamped in force at the port of Ascalon. The story goes that Raymond was first offered the crown, but he refused it, probably because he realized he was not the popular choice. He said that he would not wear a crown of gold in the city where Jesus wore the crown of

وتحمل القفص والجمل والفرس والإبلة أنها لضغت علي بالله فأضاعت بعض منزلجها

ونشد من زرجهما لما أني وزنت بالرقعة درهما وقطعة وقلت لها أرغبت في المشوف المعلم

واسرن الجب الدرهم فوجي بالسر المبهم وإن ابان نرجي فخذي القطعة وآبرزت

قالت الى اسطلاض البدر التم والأبلغ الهمر وقالت دع جدالك نبلع عابدالك فاسطع

طلع الشيخ ولدبه والشع نرده فتاين ان الشخ من أهليه وج وهو الذي وني

From a thirteenth-century Arab book illustration, the procession at the end of Ramadan, the ninth month of the Islamic year, a time of prayer and fasting thorns. He may have intended to make it impossible for Godfrey to accept the crown, but Godfrey sidestepped the issue by agreeing to become ruler without adopting the title of king.

The Battle of Ascalon

Most of the crusaders felt that they had liberated Jerusalem and completed their pilgrimage, and it was now time to return home. But they postponed their departure to join the new ruler as he marched out to meet the Egyptian army. The battle was fought on August 12, 1099, and like the battle of Antioch, the odds were so overwhelmingly against the crusaders that their victory seemed miraculous. They took the Holy Lance found at Antioch into battle again and also a fragment of the Holy Cross that a Christian inhabitant of Jerusalem had supposedly concealed during the Saracen occupation.

They were also helped by an enemy trick that misfired. The Saracens herded a lot of cattle and sheep onto the plain between the two armies in an attempt to lure soldiers away from the ranks of the army. The crusaders' leaders warned them against plundering the herds. When they went into battle, they found that the animals kept pace with them, advancing when they advanced and halting when they halted. The marching herds kicked up such a cloud of dust that the Saracens thought the crusader army was much larger than it actually was, and the dust concealed its movements. The Saracens were defeated.

And so, three years after they had set out from western Europe, the crusaders could say they had reached their objective by securing Jerusalem for their fellow Christians. It was

The siege of Antioch, from a twelfth-century French illuminated manuscript

an amazing achievement. Looking back, we can see now that they were very lucky to strike when they did. Had they launched their campaign twenty years earlier or twenty years later, they would have met much stronger resistance from the Turks, who were very disunited when the crusaders arrived in their lands. It is no wonder that the Christians felt their god was favoring them. But the cost of their victory had been enormous. Thousands of crusaders had died, not to mention thousands more Muslims, Jews, and eastern Christians who were also killed.

Now the crusaders who remained had to look to the future. Many, both leaders and soldiers, completed their pilgrimage by visiting the holy places in Jerusalem and then sailed for home before winter set in. This was what they had always intended to do. But it left the new ruler, Godfrey, pitifully short of men to defend the new conquest and to secure the surrounding territory. It seems that no one had really thought about what would happen once Jerusalem was captured. Ironically, Pope Urban, who had launched the expedition in 1095, died two weeks after the conquest, without knowing about the success of the enterprise.

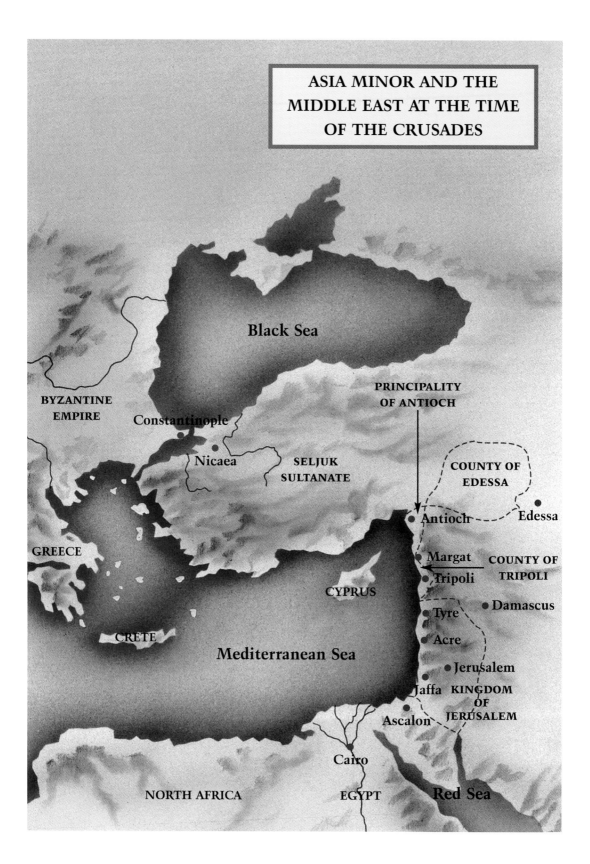

ASIA MINOR AND THE
MIDDLE EAST AT THE TIME
OF THE CRUSADES

Black Sea

BYZANTINE
EMPIRE

Constantinople

Nicaea

SELJUK
SULTANATE

PRINCIPALITY
OF ANTIOCH

COUNTY OF
EDESSA

Antioch

Edessa

GREECE

Margat

Tripoli

COUNTY OF
TRIPOLI

CYPRUS

Damascus

Tyre

Acre

CRETE

Mediterranean Sea

Jerusalem

Jaffa

KINGDOM
OF
JERUSALEM

Ascalon

Cairo

NORTH AFRICA

EGYPT

Red Sea

Glossary

abbot   Head of a community of monks.

Asia Minor   The part of Asia that is nearest to Europe, on the other side of the straits from Constantinople (modern-day Istanbul).

bishops   Christian priest in position of authority.

Byzantine Empire   The Eastern Roman Empire established in the fourth century AD by the emperor Constantine, which survived the destruction of the Roman Empire in the West and was ruled by Greek-speaking emperors.

cleric   Man who has taken a vow of religion; priest.

Constantinople   Capital of the Byzantine Empire, situated where Europe and Asia meet (modern-day Istanbul).

Crusade   Christian expeditions against nonbelievers during the Middle Ages.

Franks   People who lived in the area of modern France, but also a wider region including parts of the Low Countries and modern Germany; often used at this time for all western Europeans.

garrison   Soldiers stationed in a town to protect it.

knight Originally any soldier on horseback, but by the time of the First Crusade, a term used for men of high social status.

lance A long, pointed weapon made of wood, used by knights when charging on horseback.

peasant Person who worked in the fields and lived in the countryside (the great majority of medieval people).

penance A hardship undertaken by a Christian to make amends for sins and to obtain forgiveness.

Persia A powerful empire that opposed the Byzantines in the fifth and sixth centuries.

pilgrimage A journey made for religious reasons to a place considered holy.

pope The bishop of Rome, recognized by western Christians as head of their church.

relic The body part or possession of a holy person that was a focus of reverence for believers.

Saracens Muslims of Egypt who opposed the Turks.

Seljuk Turks Tribal warriors from central Asia who had been converted to Islam in the eleventh century.

siege When an army tries to force the defenders of a fortified place to surrender.

squire A knight's attendant, usually aspiring to knighthood himself.

truce An agreed upon cessation of warfare for a limited period

vassal Holder of land from a lord in return for an oath of homage (obedience).

For More Information

The Columbia University Medieval Guild
602 Philosophy Hall
Columbia University
New York, NY 10027
e-mail: cal36@columbia.edu
Web site: http://www.cc.Columbia.edu/cu/medieval

The Dante Society of America
Brandeis University
P.O. Box 549110
Waltham, MA 02454-9110
e-mail: dsa@dantesociety.org
Web site: http://www.dantesociety.org/index.htm

International Courtly Literature Society
North American Branch
c/o Sara Sturm-Maddox
Department of French and Italian
University of Massachusetts at Amherst
Amherst, MA 01003
e-mail: ssmaddox@frital.umass.edu
Web site: http://www-dept.usm.edu/~engdept/icls/
    iclsnab.htm

Medieval Academy of America
1430 Massachusetts Avenue
Cambridge, MA 02138
(617) 491-1622
e-mail: speculum@medievalacademy.org
Web site: http://www.medievalacademy.org/t_bar_2.htm

Rocky Mountain Medieval and Renaissance Association
Department of English Language and Literature
University of Northern Iowa
Cedar Falls, IA 50614-0502
(319) 273-2089
e-mail: jesse.swan@uni.edu
Web site: http://www.uni.edu/~swan/rmmra/rocky.htm

Web Sites

Due to the changing nature of Internet links, the Rosen
Publishing Group, Inc., has developed an online list of
Web sites related to the subject of this book. This site is
updated regularly. Please use this link to access the list:

http://www.rosenlinks.com/lma/ficr

For Further Reading

Hamilton, Bernard. *The Crusades*. Stroud, England: Sutton Publishing, 1998.

Jones, Terry, and Alan Ereira. *Crusades*. London: BBC Books, 1994.

Madden, Thomas F. *A Concise History of the Crusades*. New York: Rowman and Littlefield, 1999.

Nicolle, David. *The Crusades and the Crusader States*. Elite Series No. 19. London: Osprey Publishing, 1988.

Severin, Tim. *Crusader: By Horse to Jerusalem*. London: Hutchinson, 1989.

Tate, Georges. *The Crusades and the Holy Land*. New York: Harry N. Abrams, 1996.

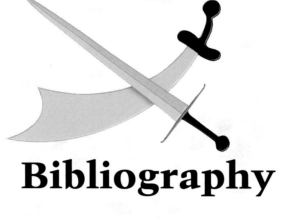

Bibliography

Baldwin, Marshall W., ed. *A History of the Crusades: The First Hundred Years.* Wisconsin History of the Crusades, gen. ed. Kenneth M. Setton, Vol. 1. Madison: University of Wisconsin Press, 1969.

Chazan, Robert. *In the Year 1096: The First Crusade and the Jews.* Philadelphia: The Jewish Publication Society, 1996.

France, John. *Victory in the East: A Military History of the First Crusade.* Cambridge, England: Cambridge University Press, 1994.

Hallam, Elizabeth, ed. *Chronicles of the Crusades.* New York: Weidenfeld & Nicholson, 1989.

Hillenbrand, Carole. *The Crusades: Islamic Perspectives.* Edinburgh: Edinburgh University Press, 1999.

Maalouf, Amin. *The Crusades Through Arab Eyes.* London: Al Saqi Books, 1984.

Peters, Edward, ed. *The First Crusade: The Chronicle of Fulcher of Chartres and Other Source Materials.* 2nd ed. Philadelphia: University of Pennsylvania Press, 1998.

Phillips, Jonathan, ed. *The First Crusade: Origins and Impact.* New York: Manchester University Press, 1997.

Riley-Smith, Jonathan, ed. *The Atlas of the Crusades.* London: Times Books, 1990.

Riley-Smith, Jonathan, ed. *The Oxford Illustrated History of the Crusades.* Oxford, England: Oxford University Press, 1995.

Runciman, Steven. *A History of the Crusades 1: The First Crusade.* Cambridge, England: Cambridge University Press, 1951.

Index

About the Author

Susan Edgington has taught adult education courses for thirty years, while maintaining an active research interest in the Crusades. She has written many books and articles, most recently *Gendering the Crusades* (with Sarah Lambert, University of Wales Press, 2001). She is currently working on a book about crusader medicine. Besides continuing to lecture at Huntingdonshire Regional College, Dr. Edgington is a visiting lecturer at Queen Mary, University of London, and a research associate of the Open University.

Photo Credits

Designer: Geri Giordano; **Editor:** Jake Goldberg; **Photo Researcher:** Elizabeth Loving